Kanji de Manga
Special Edition

YOJIJUKUGO

D1015406

MANGA UNIVERSITY presents...

YOJIJUKUGO

Created by Glenn Kardy   Art by Chihiro Hattori

Japanime
TOKYO   SAN FRANCISCO

Manga University Presents ... Kanji de Manga Special Edition: Yojijukugo

Published by Manga University under the auspices of Japanime Co. Ltd., 3-31-18 Nishi-Kawaguchi, Kawaguchi-shi, Saitama-ken 332–0021, Japan.

www.mangauniversity.com

First edition, April 2008

ISBN-13: 978-4-921205-22-5
ISBN-10: 4-921205-22-1

10 9 8 7 6 5 4 3 2 1   y 15 14 13 12 11 10 09 08

Printed in Canada

CONTENTS

The Manga University
Mission Statement

The mission of Manga University is to enlighten and educate the international community on all aspects of Japanese culture through the creative use of traditional manga artwork.

The university recognizes that manga transcends mainstream entertainment and possesses a unique ability to convey the true spirit of Japan, making the art form an ideal communicative tool to touch the lives and inspire the minds of Japan enthusiasts worldwide.

Our mission and philosophy are firmly rooted in the principles and conviction of the Japanese educational tradition and in the best ideals of Japanese heritage.

Founded at the turn of the century and located in Tokyo, Manga University is one of the world's foremost publishers of manga-themed educational materials.

FOREWORD

Welcome to the most challenging — and rewarding — course Manga University has ever offered. We're going to take you deep inside the world of 四字熟語 (yojijukugo), four-kanji expressions that make up some of the best-known and loved Japanese idioms.

Many people who have visited Japan over the years have found that the use of simple, everyday phrases is often rewarded with ooohs, ahhs and comments like 上手ですね！(じょうずですね！, or you're so good!) as if the speaker had just delivered a grand lecture in Japanese. But you know you've 立身出世 (りっしんしゅっせ, or made a name for yourself) when people stop talking about how well you speak — and simply talk to you as they would to another Japanese.

Learning these yojijukugo expressions and working them into your conversations and writing will help you get to that point and bring you closer to your goal of fluency in the Japanese language.

Of course, there are different levels of fluency. Many people are happy enough just to be conversational, and they will continue to hear those compliments about how well they speak Japanese. But Manga University students are a far different breed. You are here because you want to read and write as well as you speak, and do so like a native Japanese.

There are times when that may feel like an 悪戦苦闘 (あくせんくとう, or an uphill battle), but hard work and dedication can help get you there. And we'll help get you there, too. That touch of fun you've come to expect from Manga University will turn 支離滅裂 (しりめつれつ, or gobbledygook) into expressions you can use every day.

Technically, any expression with four kanji can be called a yojijukugo. However, we are going to focus more specifically on idiomatic four-kanji compounds, many of which have been in use for centuries — but still sound as fresh and natural as if they were coined yesterday.

The faculty here at Manga University have always taken pride in honesty. And the honest truth is that these can be challenging for non-native speakers to master and work into their everyday speech.

However, we take an equal amount of pride in our ability to transform linguistic challenges into a lively and fun course that will not only break everything down so it's easy to understand, but allow you to enjoy the process of learning as well.

By this point, you are no doubt 興味津津 (きょうみしんしん, or brimming with curiosity) about these expressions — so let's get started. Study them. Learn them. Commit them to memory. But more importantly, use them — and enjoy them!

INTRODUCTION

You are holding in your hands something unique. *Kanji de Manga Special Edition: Yojijukugo* is not only a fun way to learn Japanese through manga, but the first book to truly deliver an accessible way for English speakers to learn 四字熟語 (よじじゅくご, yojijukugo), or four-character idioms and expressions.

YOJI-WHAT NOW?

So what are yojijukugo? Well, the broadest explanation is any word or expression that is made up of four 漢字 (かんじ, kanji), or Chinese characters. As you may know, kanji often represent one broad word or concept, (for example, 漢, kan, meaning "Han-Chinese"; and 字, ji, meaning "character") but when combined can form compounds that represent more specific ideas (漢字: "Chinese characters"). What makes yojijukugo so special, however, is not the number of characters, but what they can express in such a concise manner.

In general, most yojijukugo are expressions that stem from ancient Chinese *chengyu,* or set phrases, though some of their meanings have changed over time to reflect more modern ideas. There are also plenty of yojijukugo that originated with Japanese language, and even today new yojijukugo are occasionally created.

TWO OF A KIND

There are two kinds of yojijukugo: those that have just one simple definition; and those that are idiomatic expressions with broad meanings. An example of the first kind of yojijukugo would be:

焼肉定食　（やきにくていしょく）

The first kanji (焼) means "grilled."
The second kanji (肉) means "meat."
The third and fourth kanji (定食) together mean "a set meal," so the whole conjunction together basically means "a grilled meat value meal." There are literally thousands of these non-idiomatic expressions, and while they do fall under the category "yojijukugo," they have simple, straightfoward definitions, and so this book does not cover them.

An idiomatic yojijukugo is a four-character word or expression that may have originally had only one meaning, but has come to represent a broad and often profound expression or proverb. For example:

一石二鳥（いっせきにちょう）

The first kanji (一) is the number "one."
The second kanji (石) means "stone."
The third kanji (二) is the number "two."
The fourth kanji (鳥) means "bird."
The literal meaning of this yojijukugo should sound familiar: "kill two birds with one stone." In all likelihood this expression originated when people killed birds with stones for food, but now

any situation where you can take care of two things by doing only one thing.

Because of the elegant simplicity of yojijukugo, they are seen as very concise and eloquent when used in place of a more colloquial phrase, and are ideal for someone who wants to speak or write polished Japanese. At the same time, while Japanese children study yojijukugo in school, English speakers rarely learn them, even at a college level. Like slang, having a knowledge of yojijukugo shows that your Japanese know-how goes far beyond the classroom.

All of the yojijukugo in this book are idiomatic expressions that can be used in a variety of situations in both spoken and written Japanese. Many of the phrases in this book can be found in newspapers and on TV shows. Often yojijukugo are also used as titles for movies, books, blogs and more. And nothing will make a Japanese speech or essay sound more thought out than a well-placed yojijukugo.

HOW TO USE THIS BOOK

While mastering the use of yojijukugo involves writing lots of kanji, they are just as useful in conversation, so you can get a lot of mileage by learning just one. So don't get discouraged if you can't memorize them all in one go!

Start by looking at the kanji that make up the yojijukugo and learn how to recognize the compound and how it is pronounced. All of the expressions have their pronunciation written underneath them in hiragana, and there's a kana guide in the back of the book if you're feeling rusty.

Read the explanation of each individual kanji, and if there are certain characters that you don't know or are interested in, knowing a yojijukugo that uses it will help you remember in the future.

Once you get the full meaning of the yojijukugo, check out the example sentence at the bottom of the page, and think of other situations where you might use the same expression. The more you try to use the expression in your own conversation and writing, the quicker you will be able to remember it.

Many of the yojijukugo in this book also have a rich historical background as to why they have a certain meaning. We tried to include as much of this as possible because the more information you have, the easier it will be to remember new words. And knowing where a word comes from is not only helpful, it's fun! In fact, some of the things you're about to learn go well beyond what's included in yojijukugo books produced for the Japanese themselves. Excited? Great! Let's 猪突猛進 (ちょとつもうしん, charge headlong) into your first yojijukugo!

PAGE
GUIDE

① The featured yojijukugo (written in kanji).

② English definition

③ Pronunciation (written in hiragana).

④ Shows where the yojijukugo falls in the syllabary order. Use this to find a yojijukugo by its first syllable).

Japanese is "alphabetized" first in what is called 行 (ぎょう) order, which is the order of syllable types: あ、か、さ、た、な、は、ま、や、ら、わ; then, within these sets the syllables go in 段 (だん) order: あいうえお、かきくけこ etc.

⑤ The manga. Each panel illustrates the yojijukugo on that page.

⑥ An explanation of the yojijukugo, how it relates to the manga panel, examples of how it can be used, and a breakdown of each kanji in the phrase.

⑦ An example sentence that uses the yojijukugo. Everything but the selected yojijukugo is written in either hiragana or katakana, so no prior kanji experience is necessary (but it helps!).

④ さしすせそ
② Gobbledygook
① 支離滅裂
③ し　り　めつ　れつ

⑥ blagh! Yigrblrgrg! Norborgorb! No matter how you pronounce it, it's about much Japanese as it is English. Sometimes, being a native speaker just won't help. Either they can't understand you or you can't understand them, and you may as well be speaking different languages – even if you're not. The problem is, you're just speaking 支離滅裂!
The first kanji (支) means "support," or "sustain."
The second kanji (離) means "to detach," or "separate."
The third and fourth kanji (滅裂) mean "in chaos," which is what happens to your words when they turn into total gibberish! But don't worry, even world leaders have been known to devolve into 支離滅裂 every now and then.

⑦ あまりのショックで支離滅裂でなにをいっているのかわからない。
He's in such shock I can't understand the gobbledegook he's blurting out.

漢字 de マンガ

四字熟語

THE YOJIJUKUGO

悪戦苦闘

あく　せん　く　とう

Trying to move this guy is like trying to move a mountain. Not even his best judo moves can get the big guy to budge, leaving our furious fighter on the wrong side of an 悪戦苦闘. Let's take a look at just what he's up against:

The first kanji (悪) is read by itself as 悪い (わるい) and means "bad" or "wrong."

The second kanji (戦) means "war" or "battle," so when coupled with 悪 the compound means "fighting hard."

The third and fourth kanji (苦闘) together mean "agonizing," since suffering is the price of any battle. But every underdog has his day — so good luck, little guy!

じゅうどうでこどもがおとうさんをたおすのに、悪戦苦闘している。
As much as he tried to beat his dad in judo, it was an uphill battle.

Groping Blindly In The Dark

暗中模索

あん　ちゅう　も　さく

This novice could sure use a manga cookbook! Instead of learning how to brew up the perfect stew, she's just making it up at she goes along. We can only hope she doesn't expect that poor guy to sample her foul potion! This is what you get when you're 暗中模索. Let's shed a little light on it:

The first kanji (暗) is written by itself as 暗い（くらい）, which means "dark."

The second kanji (中) means "middle" or "inside."

The third and fourth kanji (模索) together mean "to search for something," so the literal translation is searching for something in the dark. In this case, a blackout is just about the only explanation for that fish-octopus-beef-carrot-banana-apple-cucumber soup!

暗中模索でりょうりするのはやめてくれ！！
Please stop trying to cook blindfolded!!

Down In The Dumps

あいうえお

意気消沈

い　き　しょう　ちん

Sometimes, you come up short no matter how hard you try. Just look at this poor guy. Even after pulling an all-nighter, he still couldn't make the grade. It's enough to get anyone 意気消沈. Let's take a closer look at what's behind that frown:

The first and second kanji（意気）together mean "spirit" or "mood."

The third kanji（消）means " extinguish" or "blow out." It can be written by itself as the verb 消す（けす）.

The fourth kanji（沈）can be used by itself as 沈む（しずむ）and means "to sink." That adds up to a perfect storm of depression... Well, time to get back on that saddle, cowboy — 明日（あした）があるさ! (Tomorrow's another day!)

テストのけっかで意気消沈している。
These test results have me really down in the dumps.

Like Pigs In A Blanket

意気投合

い　き　とう　ごう

Colleagues by day, carousers by night — these two have clearly clicked when it comes to kicking back after a hard day's work! The camaraderie shared by these fast friends can only be described as being 意気投合, and here's why:

The first and second kanji (意気) together mean "spirit" or "mood."
The third and fourth kanji (投合) together mean "unification" or "combination," so everyone can share in the good cheer. Let's hope they don't party too hard, or they may spend the next morning regretting this kanji combination! Better get those 元気（げんき）ドリンク (energy drinks) ready, just in case.

はじめてあったのに、意気投合してのみにいった。
Even though they've just met, they clicked so well they went out drinking.

Heart-To-Heart

あいうえお

以 心 伝 心

い　　しん　　でん　　しん

Ah, love... an entire language that can be spoken without words. Although the unspoken words of the heart usually need no translation, the third wheel here clearly doesn't get it. Maybe he's never had his own 以心伝心. Let's help him out:

The first kanji (以) isn't a word but a preposition: it means "by way of."
The second kanji (心) means "heart," in the spiritual sense.
The third kanji (伝) means "to communicate."
The fourth kanji (心) is "heart" again, so the phrase literally means communicating the heart, by way of the heart. Maybe their friend will get it when he finds his own manga mate!

あのカップルは以心伝心しているので、くだらないぞ～！
That couple always know what each other's thinking — how gross!

Once In A Lifetime

一期一会

あいうえお

いち　ご　いち　え

In the world of business, it's usually not what you know but who you know. So this young entrepreneur is on constant watch for new connections, and the notion of 一期一会 is on his mind each time he meets someone. After all, you never get a second chance to make a first impression. And here's why:

The first and second kanji (一期) together mean "in one's lifetime."
The third kanji (一) as in the first, this is the number "one."
The fourth kanji (会) means "to meet" or "meeting," which can mean everything from big business connections, or casual friends. 一期一会 is actually part of the Japanese title for the movie "Forrest Gump," which is filled with all those famous once-in-a-lifetime chance encounters.

はじめてのあいさつは、一期一会のきもちでやりましょう。
Make your first meeting count like it's the last one you'll ever have.

The Whole Story

一部始終

いち　ぶ　し　じゅう

Here's a woman with a plan. And she knows that before putting any plan into action, you need to step back and take another look at it from start to finish, or 一部始終. And here's the whole story behind that:

The first and second kanji (一部) together mean "one part."

The third kanji (始) means "to begin."

The fourth kanji (終) means "to end," and with 始 forms a compound meaning "from beginning to end." The last two characters are an example of a typical category of kanji compound called 対義語 (たいぎご) in which two characters with opposite meanings are written together to create a broader meaning.

きょうのぼうけんのプランを一部始終しっているのは、かのじょだけだ。
Only she knows the whole plan behind today's adventure.

As Plain As Day

一　目　瞭　然

いち　　もく　　りょう　　ぜん

What started out as a seemingly impossible task has come down to the final piece. This jigsaw junkie had no idea what would go where when he began. But now that he's down to the final piece, he can tell just by looking. You might say it's 一目瞭然. Let's examine the individual pieces of this kanji puzzle:

The first and second kanji (一目) together mean a "glance" or "one look."
The third and fourth kanji (瞭然) form a compound meaning "obvious," and that leaves our puzzle master just seconds away from gluing this one together. That's right — in Japan, finished jigsaw puzzles are often glued with a clear paste to preserve the completed work.

さいごのパズルがどこにはまるかは一目瞭然。
Where the last piece of the puzzle fits is as plain as day.

Get Rich Quick

一 攫 千 金

いっ　かく　せん　きん

Woo-hoo! Forget instant fame — most of us would rather have instant fortune. Our new friend has hit the big time, and now he's in the money. Before we hit him up for a loan — or, better still, inquire about the possibility of a "gift," — let's look inside this 一攫千金 scheme:

The first and second kanji (一攫) together mean "one grab."

The third kanji (千) means "one thousand," and is read as せん or ぜん when used in counting.

The fourth kanji (金) is one you might know better as かね. It means "gold," or "money," and there's a lot of it to be made if you hit it big in the manga game... maybe.

みんな一攫千金のゆめをみて、たからくじをかう。
It's the dream of getting rich quick that make people buy lottery tickets.

Happy One Minute, Sad the Next

一喜一憂

いっ　き　いち　ゆう

This must be one moving work of literature. She's not only engrossed by every page, but the story has her riding an emotional roller coaster. When the characters soar, he spirits rise. And when their lives take a turn for the worse, her mood turns sour. She's clearly 一喜一憂. Let's read into this one:

The first kanji (一) means "one."

The second kanji (喜) means "to take pleasure in something," and can also be written as the verb 喜ぶ(よろこぶ).

The third kanji (一) is the same as the first, the number "one."

The fourth kanji (憂) means "to be anxious," "sad" or "unhappy," and can be used by itself as 憂える(うれえる).

かのじょはチャプターごとに 一喜一憂している。
Her emotional state is changing from chapter to chapter.

Time Is Money

あいうえお

一刻千金

いっ　こく　せん　きん

This busy salaryman wastes no time during the work week. If he misses a call or meeting it could mean his job, so loafing isn't an option. While some might say money can't buy happiness, he knows money buys a lot of other things he wants, so he lives by the credo 一刻千金!

The first and second kanji (一刻) together mean "one moment" or "an instant"

The third and fourth kanji (千金) form the same compound as in 一攫千金, meaning literally "1000 pieces of gold," or "priceless," which is the going rate for even a moment of our man's precious time. Let's just hope he has time to enjoy it someday.

ごがつのれんきゅうは一刻千金なのでやすめない。
Time is money — I just can't afford to take spring vacation this May.

With All One's Might

一生懸命

いっ　しょう　けん　めい

The phrase 一生懸命 is at the very heart of the Japanese 頑張る（がんばる）spirit: the philosophy that you should do everything as best as you can. Our friend here may not be in a basket-bike marathon, but he's definitely showing us the meaning of 一生懸命 by peddling with all his might. Maybe he's just trying to get home in time for his favorite anime show.
The first and second kanji （一生）together mean "one's whole life"
The third and fourth kanji （懸命）together mean "to risk one's life," but you don't literally need to put your life at stake to do something 一生懸命. Manga artists, however, often sacrifice sleep and proper nutrition when they're hard at work.

一生懸命こげばテーマソングまでにまにあうかもしれない！
If I peddle as hard as I can I might make it in time for the theme song!

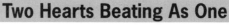
Two Hearts Beating As One

あいうえお

一心同体

いっ　しん　どう　たい

Yumiko and Kimiko aren't sisters, but they have lots in common. They spend all their time together, finish each other's sentences, and always know what the other is thinking. They get mistaken for twins all the time, but really they're just 一心同体. Let's see what these kanji have in common:

The first and second kanji (一心) together mean "wholeheartedness," and in this case "one mind."

The third kanji (同) means "the same," and you may have also seen it written as 同じ（おなじ）.

The fourth kanji (体) can also be read as からだ. It means "body," and although these girls have two of them, they may as well be sharing one!

わたしたちはいつも一心同体でまるでふたごみたい！
Our hearts are always beating as one, it's almost like we're twins!

A One-Track Mind

いっ　　　　しん　　　　ふ　　　　らん

No matter what time of day or night it is, Dr. Yamada is in the same place, doing the same thing. He's hard at work in his lab, adding a drop of this to a vial of that, searching for the right combination of ingredients that will help him escape this page and come to life! But to reach his goal he's got to be 一心不乱. Here's the formula:

The first and second kanji (一心) together mean "wholeheartedness."

The third kanji (不) isn't a word by itself, but it negates whatever comes after it.

The fourth kanji (乱) means "revolt" or "disturb," so hopefully our friend can stay focused enough not to blow up this book!

一心不乱にけんきゅうをする。
I do my research without any interruptions.

Kill Two Birds With One Stone

一　石　二　鳥

いっ　せき　に　ちょう

Sometimes even a lousy fisherman can get lucky. He would have been happy with one little fish — but today, that one little fish became bait for a much bigger fish. You might say he caught two fish with one worm, but a more traditional way of putting it is 一石二鳥. Let's see what's in his tackle box:

The first kanji (一) is the number "one."
The second kanji (石) means "stone."
The third kanji (二) is the number "two."
The fourth kanji (鳥) means "bird," and can be read as とり by itself.

Surprisingly, though this idiom dates back to ancient China, it's likely it was translated from 17th-century English!

こんなつりってあり〜？！一石二鳥じゃん！
What did I catch?! It's a two-for-one!

Cut In Two With One Stroke

一　刀　両　断

いっ　とう　りょう　だん

あいうえお

Here's a figure of speech that's probably common in your favorite samurai comic, but like any good 四字熟語, it can be used in all sorts of situations. In this case, our brave manga mom is able to step in between two bickering brothers and 一刀両断. Let's sharpen our knowledge on this one:

The first kanji (一) is the number "one."

The second kanji (刀) means "sword" or "knife," and it forms a compound with the first to mean "a single stroke."

The third and fourth kanji (両断) mean "cut in half," but we're sure the boys will eventually patch things up. If they don't, they'll have to deal with mom, but 一刀両断 can be used when moderating any two parties — not just kids!

おかあさんはこどものけんかを一刀両断する。
Mom stepped right in and put an end to the kids' bickering.

因果応報

いん　が　おう　ほう

While it's no fun to save your money while everyone else is out spending their allowances, it helps to keep the bigger picture in mind. At the end of the season Chihiro will be sitting pretty on a nice, big pile of cash, with her 因果応報 attitude to thank for it. Let's break open this piggy bank:

The first kanji (因) means "cause"

The second kanji (果) means "finish" or "carry out," so it forms a 対義語 compound with the first to mean "cause and effect" or "karma."

The third and fourth kanji (応報) together mean "retribution," so take care to do unto others as you would have them do unto you, or this karmic kanji combination will come back to bite you!

じぶんのおこないは因果応報でかえってくる。
Your actions will eventually come back to haunt you.

Don't Know If You're Coming Or Going

右往左往

う　おう　さ　おう

あいうえお

Should he or shouldn't he? This way or that way? Clearly, this is one confused young man. Each time he thinks he's made up his mind, he changes it and heads in the other direction. His dilemma can best be summed up in Japanese as 右往左往. Let's see if we can point him in the right direction:

The first kanji (右) means "right."
The second kanji (往) means "going."
The third kanji (左) means "left."
The fourth kanji (往) is the same as the second, "going." With characters like that dancing around, no wonder he can't figure out what to do!

いつまでもけつだんができず右往左往。
I can never decide, I just keep going back and fourth.

Golden Age

黄 金 時 代

おう　　ごん　　じ　　だい

How many times has your potbellied おじさん (uncle) regaled you with stories about being a teenaged heartthrob during his "wonder years"? Everyone deserves a moment to think back to their 黄金時代, but don't you wonder why the girls' names change every time he retells the story? Let's give him a kanji reality check:

The first and second kanji (黄金) together mean "gold" or "golden."
The third and fourth kanji (時代) together mean "period," "epoch" or "era," and the phrase can apply to everything from art to sports or even politics — not just long-ago high school romances that maybe never happened.

だれでも黄金時代があったはず。
I guess everyone has their golden age, right?

Out Of Touch

音信不通

おん　しん　ふ　つう

あいうえお

Face it, kiddo — he's gone. He hasn't called, written or even sent a single lousy text message. But Yukino still sits and and stares at that photograph, hoping that he hasn't really left — he's just 音信不通. Let's find out why he's so hard to reach:

The first and second kanji (音信) together mean "correspondence."

The third kanji (不) isn't a word by itself, but it negates whatever comes after it.

The fourth kanji (通) means "to pass through," so it forms a compound with 不 that means "interruption" or "suspension." Yukino may be alone, but at least she's got plenty of kanji to help keep her mind busy!

わたしのかれしは、りゅうがくしてから音信不通・・・しくしく。
Ever since my boyfriend went abroad he's been completely out of touch... sniff.

The Great Outdoors

花　鳥　風　月

か　　ちょう　　ふう　　げつ

Sometimes you've got to break out of that stuffy office and experience all nature has to offer. The fresh air... the wind in your hair... it's been known to cause some people to break out into song. That's the power of Mother Nature when you visit 花鳥風月.

The first kanji (花) means "flower."

The second kanji (鳥) means "bird."

The third kanji (風) means "wind."

The fourth kanji (月) means "moon." 花鳥風月 is part of a special category of idioms that combine four kanji with unique but related meanings (in this case, kanji that refer to nature) to form a broader meaning.

あ〜やっぱりつかれたときは、花鳥風月にかこまれるのがいちばんだわ！

Aaah... When you're feeling run down, being in the Great Outdoors is the best!

Looking Out For Number One

が　でん　いん　すい

かきくけこ

He's got his nose deep in the latest shonen manga, and believe it or not, that's what caught the eye of this feisty female. She's told him that only a true otaku can be her knight in shining armor. Too bad for him she has a 我田引水 policy: She takes what she wants, when she wants it.

The first kanji （我）means "oneself."
The second kanji （田）means "field."
The third kanji （引）means "to pull."
The fourth kanji （水）means "water." so the literal meaning of the phrase is "to draw water to one's field," no doubt originally a reference to a selfish farmer.

かってにきめるなんて我田引水だ〜！
You can't just "choose" a husband; how selfish can you get!

The Finishing Touch

画 竜 点 睛

が　りょう　てん　せい

Japanese domino champion Taoshi Tarou is about to complete his newest, longest, and most incredible setup yet. Sweat dripping from his brow, all that remains is to very carefully insert the final piece, or 画竜点睛. Let's watch:

The first kanji (画) means "a painting" or "brushstroke."

The second kanji (竜) means "dragon."

The third kanji (点) means "a spot" or "mark."

The fourth kanji (睛) means "pupil," as the literal meaning of the phrase is "to dot the eyes of a painted dragon," which according to ancient Chinese art practices was typically the last step in painting dragons. Somehow, though, we don't think our domino champ wants to be distracted by historical trivia just now.

いきをころして画竜点睛をする。
Hold your breath as you add the finishing touch.

感慨無量

かん　がい　む　りょう

A great movie can really cause your emotions to spill out of you. This theatergoer has clearly just experienced one of those movies, an anime film so powerful it caused him to be 感慨無量. Let's compose ourselves just long enough to examine this one:

The first and second kanji (感慨) together mean "strong feelings."

The third kanji (無) like 不, is not a word but a particle, and it means "none."

The fourth kanji (量) means "amount," so it forms a compound with 無 that means "immeasurable." It's a good thing that advertisers in Japan pass out tissue packets in the street instead of fliers — this guy's gonna need a whole bunch!

ふつうはなかないけど、このえいがは感慨無量だった～！
I usually don't cry, but that film moved me to tears!

A Close Shave

危　機　一　髪

き　き　いっ　ぱつ

Yowzers! That could've hurt somebody! Whoever lives above here has got to be more careful when they throw vases off the balcony. Luckily, they missed the target by a hair — it was just a 危機一髪. Beware of these four characters:

The first and second kanji (危機) together mean "crisis."
The third kanji (一) is our familiar friend, the number "one."
The fourth kanji (髪) means "hair," so danger is definitely within a hair's breadth. Hopefully our friend will exercise caution by learning a few more kanji: 落石に注意 (watch for falling rocks)! 危機一髪 doesn't always have to refer to something that is life-threatening, either; a close call on a test at school, or nearly forgetting a friend's birthday can be just as ぎりぎり (nail-biting)!

ギャー危機一髪だった！はぁしぬかとおもった！
Whoa, that missed me by a hair! I thought I was a goner!

Beginning, Middle, Climax, End

かきくけこ

起　承　転　結

き　　しょう　　てん　　けつ

This 四字熟語 has its roots in early Japanese and Chinese literature, with each character representing a piece of a story. Today, any manga story will follow this pattern, as our banana-peel man proves. Here's an outline:

The first kanji (起) means "to wake up."
The second kanji (承) means "to be informed."
The third kanji (転) means "to turn around."
The fourth kanji (結) means "to tie up." Having a beginning, middle, climax and an end to any story of course goes far beyond Asian literature: Pretty much any decent plotline will follow this structure, too. Also, like 花鳥風月, this idiom is another where four distinct words form a broader concept.

アニメをつくるときに、だいじなことは起承転結をかんがえることである。
When you make anime, it's important to think out the entire story.

疑 心 暗 鬼

ぎ　　し　ん　　あ　ん　　き

Even on a perfectly peaceful evening, Hikaru can't help but think the worst of everyone she passes — even the neighbor's pooch! She should talk to a shrink about 疑心暗鬼. You can't learn new phrases if you're afraid of the unknown:

The first kanji（疑）means "to doubt" or "be suspicious."

The second kanji（心）means "heart" or "spirit," and forms a compound with 疑 that means "apprehension."

The third kanji（暗）means "darkness."

The fourth kanji（鬼）means "devil" or "demon," so the phrase literally means "to be apprehensive of demons in the darkness." Of course, everyone knows there's no such things as ghosts... wait — what's that *behind you!?!?*

サスペンスをみたあとは疑心暗鬼になって、そとにでるのがこわい！
After watching a thriller I'm so scared to go outside, I jump at the shadows!

Out Of This World

奇想天外

き　そう　てん　がい

Abracadabra! Hocus-Pocus! Shazam! No matter how many times you see the levitation trick in person, it's always 奇想天外. Let's learn these magic words:

The first kanji (奇) means "strange" or "curious."
The second kanji (想) means "thought" or "idea."
The third kanji (天) means "heaven."
The fourth kanji (外) means "outside," so it forms a compound with 天 that means "beyond the heavens." OK, so these kanji don't exactly add up to "alakazam," and won't help you levitate your friends or pull a bunny out of a hat, but just being able to read and write them is definitely 奇想天外 to most Westerners!

たしかに奇想天外におもえるけど、トリックがあるはず。
It sure looks out of this world, but there's got to be some sort of trick to it.

喜 怒 哀 楽

き ど あい らく

Who says boys don't cry? It's natural for a healthy, well balanced manga character to be able to express all of their emotions on paper and as you can see, Fujiwara here can go through the whole range of 喜怒哀楽. Let's see how this 四字熟語 makes you feel:

The first kanji (喜) means "joy," or "delight"
The second kanji (怒) means "anger"
The third kanji (哀) means "sorrow"
The fourth kanji (楽) means "comfort." In English there's no one phrase that encompasses the entire range of human emotions, but in Japanese, you can use a 四字熟語 like this to spell out exactly what you mean.

あなたのせいかくは、なんて喜怒哀楽がはげしいのだろう。
It's just your personality to have really violent mood swings.

Near-Death Experience

九　死　一　生

きゅう　　し　　いっ　　しょう

Boom! A car erupts into flames in the middle of a crowded street. The driver drags himself from the wreckage, narrowly escaping the jaws of death. A man in a dark suit who's watched the whole event transpire from a safe distance mumbles "九死一生." Let's look at the police report:

The first kanji (九) is the number "nine"

The second kanji (死) means "death," and forms a compound with the first kanji meaning someone's death is just short of certain, or "9 out of 10."

The third and fourth kanji (一生) together mean "one's whole life," which was probably what flashed before the eyes of this accident victim.

あのじこからにげられたなんて、まるで九死一生。
I can't believe I made it out of that accident — what a brush with death.

A Swift Resolution

急 転 直 下

きゅう　てん　ちょっ　か

Notorious burglar Mustache Jiro was on the loose, and it looked like the police were never going to find him — until he walked right by his own wanted poster! This 急転直下 was a lucky break for the boys in blue, but can you pick the right kanji out from the lineup?:

The first kanji (急) means "hurry" or "sudden."

The second kanji (転) means "turn around" or "change," so it combines with 急 to mean "sudden change."

The third kanji (直) means "honesty," but can mean "directly" in some cases.

The fouth kanji (下) means "below," so when added to 直 it means a change in events is just under your nose — or in this case, just under a poster!

みんなのつうほうで、急転直下にくちひげじろうがつかまった。
With everyone's cooperation we were able to aprehend Mustache Jiro right away.

Wolfing It Down

牛　飲　馬　食

ぎゅう　いん　ば　しょく

He may not be six-time hot dog eating champion Takeru Kobayashi, but he's well on his way! Competitive eating is actually a pretty good way to gain celebrity in Japan, so even though 牛飲馬食 may be something your parents scoff at, it could pay the bills if you've got the skills! Here's our menu today:

The first kanji (牛) means "cow."
The second kanji (飲) means "to drink."
The third kanji (馬) means "horse."
The fourth kanji (食) means "to eat," so while similar to the Engish idiom "wolfing it down," the Japanese phrase uses different animals to get its point across. Now, go ahead, it's OK — make a pig (or cow or horse) of yourself!

ただおくんは牛飲馬食だから、おおぐいコンテストでゆうしょうまちがいないね。
Tadao-kun really wolfs it down, he's a shoe-in for the eating contest!

共存共栄

きょう　ぞん　きょう　えい

Normally, cats and mice don't get along so well. After all, a cat-and-mouse game is usually just a game for the cat. But these guys have worked out a different kind of relationship. The cat protects the mice, and in return the mice attend to his every need. Here's how these characters coexist:

The first kanji (共) means "together."

The second kanji (存) means "to be aware of," and forms a compound with the first kanji to mean "coexistence."

The third kanji (共) is the same as the first, again meaning "together."

The fourth kanji (栄) means "prosperity," which is what both parties hope to achieve in a 共存共栄.

このどうぶつみたいに、にんげんもせんそうしないで共存共栄すればいいよにゃー！
If only humans could end war and live in perfect harmony like these critters... meow!

Brimming With Curiosity

興味津津

きょう　み　しん　しん

It's probably no surprise that like their counterparts around the world, most Japanese boys are crazy about bugs. This boy, however, is taking his entomological hobby to a whole new level. Armed with his trusty magnifying glass, he's going after every insect he can find - he's simply 興味津津. Let's satisfy our own curiosity about this expression:

The first and second kanji (興味) form a very common compound that means "interest."

The third and fourth kanji (津津) are the same, and mean "harbor" by themselves, but written together they mean "brimful," or "being full." A kanji that is repeated is usually written as 々 but here it helps to see the kanji twice!

こどもってなんでも興味津津だね！
Children are always just brimming with interest, no matter what the subject!

Unspeakably Bad

言語道断

かきくけこ

げん　ご　どう　だん

Talk about your bad days... Or maybe you'd rather not talk about them at all. This guy's been scratched by a cat, had his favorite boot carried away by a seagull, was splashed by a speeding car, and the list goes on! Sometimes things are so bad you just can't find the words to describe them, but we've found the kanji: 言語道断. Maybe it won't be so unspeakable if we break it down:

The first and second kanji (言語) form a compound that means "language."
The third kanji (道) means "road" or "way."
The fourth kanji (断) means "cutting" or "severance," so this poor guy is simply at a loss for words.

きょうはおみくじのとおりに言語道断のいちにちだった。
Today was just as rotten as my fortune said it would be.

Barefaced Impudence

厚 顔 無 恥

こう　がん　む　ち

The Japanese can be sticklers for manners when it comes to how people are expected to behave on the train. But come on, lady, some of the rules are just common sense! When your big bottom takes up the space of three people and then you just sit there passing gas unapologetically, people are bound to say you've got 厚顔無恥. Let's have the good manners to learn this one:

The first and second kanji (厚顔) form a compound meaning "impudence."
The third kanji (無) is not a word but a particle, and it means "none," and is often used when a suffix like "-less" might appear (in this case "shameless")
The fourth kanji (恥) means "shame," a word this rude rider apparently hasn't heard of!

あんなせまいスペースにすわろうなんて厚顔無恥なひとだ。
How rude of her to try to squeeze into such a narrow space!

かきくけこ

広 大 無 辺

こう　だい　む　へん

Taking a breath of fresh air at the seashore can be a nice change from the stale air of the city, refreshing not just your lungs but your spirit, too. Bring your kanji books to the beach and experience 広大無辺. These are your tickets to freedom:

The first kanji (広) means "wide" or "spacious."

The second kanji (大) means "big," so it forms a compound with the first character that means "vast," or "extensive."

The third kanji (無) is not a word but a particle, and it means "none."

The fourth kanji (辺) means "boundary," or "border," so you can connect it to 無 it to mean "boundless."

せまいオフィスから広大無辺なうみにくると、じゆうなかんじがする。
To go from a cramped office to the endless ocean really makes you feel free.

Fair Play

公平無私

こう　へい　む　し

You may think that 公平無私 is the edict of a sports referee, but It's even more important to a mother of twins! Nothing will keep these two brothers from fighting like a pair of hockey players better than a mom that knows never to play favorites. These kanji are the secret to her harmonious home:

The first kanji (公) means "public."

The second kanji (平) means "peace," and forms a compound with the first kanji to mean "fairness."

The third kanji (無) is not a word but a particle, and it means "none."

The fourth kanji (私) means "I" or "me" and with 無 forms a compound that means "unselfish." Hopefully, both of these boys will grow up to agree with that!

ココアにおなじかずのマシュマロをいれることは公平無私だわ。
I put the same number of marshmallows into each cup of cocoa, it's only fair.

Young And Old, Near And Far

かきくけこ

古今東西
こ　きん　とう　ざい

Some of the most popular manga take place outside of Japan. The best artists use their craft to explore different cultures, customs, and time-periods, making their art the 古今東西 medium that it is. Of course, they all have one thing in common — kanji!:

The first kanji (古) means "old."
The second kanji (今) you may know as いま, and it means "now."
The third kanji (東) means "east," and is also pronounced ひがし.
The fourth kanji (西) means "west," and is also pronounced にし.

古今東西 is another 対義語 where opposite words are matched up in order to make a broader meaning; literally, "Of all times and places."

まんがはげんざい古今東西どこにもひろがりつつある。
Manga is currently expanding to all people and places, young and old, near and far.

Diabolical

極 悪 非 道

ごく　あく　ひ　どう

Some people exude confidence. Others ooze charm. But this creep gives off something else entirely. Clearly, he wants you to know he's 極悪非道. Let's look into this heart of darkness:

The first kanji（極）means "extreme" or "the highest rank."

The second kanji（悪）means "bad" or "wrong," and forms a compound with 極 that means "heinous."

The third kanji（非）is similar to "non-" and negates whatever comes after it.

The fourth kanji（道）usually means "road" or "path" by itself, but it can also mean a moral or teaching, as in 武士道、（ぶしどう, the teachings of the ways of the samurai). There's nothing honorable about 極悪非道, though!

あのはいゆうは極悪非道でゆうめいだけど、ほんとうはやさしいパパだよね。
That actor is famous for playing nasty villains, but he's actually a sweet, caring parent.

かきくけこ

小　春　日　和
こ　はる　び　より

Weather it's an Indian summer day or a pleasantly warm winter afternoon, a 小春日和 can be enjoyed by humans and feline's alike. As long as it feels like spring even though it's not, you can use these kanji, but let's check the weather report first:

The first and second kanji (小春) literally mean "a little bit of spring," but are almost never used this way outside of this 四字熟語.

The third and fourth kanji (日和) Form a compound that's used for describing the state of the weather, so you could say 小春日和 is also the ideal ピクニック日和 (picnic weather). In addition, using 小春日和 in the winter has the connotation that spring is on its way, and you can't wait for it any longer!

にんげんでも、ねこでも、てんきがわりといい小春日和はきもちがいいね。
Both humans and cats can enjoy the unusually good weather of Indian summer.

Tooting Your Own Horn

自 画 自 賛
じ が じ さん

さしすせそ

Everyone knows Yuki is a hit with the boys, an "A" student and a top athlete... because she insists on telling everyone she meets! Maybe she needs a lesson in the offensiveness of 自画自賛 and realize that getting compliments is better than giving them to yourself.

The first kanji (自) means "onself."

The second kanji (画) means "brushstroke" and "picture," and it connects to 自 to mean "self-portrait." You may aslo recognize this kanji as the が in the word 漫画 (まんが).

The third kanji (自) is the same as the first.

The fourth kanji (賛) means to "approve" or "praise."

かのじょのいっていることは、ほんとうかどうかわからないほど自画自賛だ。
She's toots her own horn so much, I never known whether she's telling the truth.

Self-Sufficient

自 給 自 足

じ　きゅう　じ　そく

In Japan, packages of organic vegetables often feature manga drawings of the farmer that grew the fresh, delicious produce for you. Usually they don't look this young or energetic, but the Japanese commend them nonetheless for living a life that's 自給自足. But don't worry, you don't have to be 自給自足 when it comes to figuring this out – we'll help you out here:

The first and second kanji (自給) make up a compound word that means "self-support," with 給 meaning "salary" or "wages" on its own.

The third and fourth kanji (自足) together mean "self-sufficiency" or "self-satisfaction," with 足 by itself meaning "to be sufficient" (although it is also the counter word for footwear).

なつやすみはいなかで自給自足のたいけんをする。
I'm going to spend summer break in the country trying to live a self-sufficient life.

Anachronistic

時代錯誤
じ　だい　さく　ご

さしすせそ

Japan is in many ways quite forgiving of people who cling to tradition. But it's possible even in this environment to be a little too traditional. Just check out this guy, who decided to wear his shogun robes and topknot hairstyle. He's become a walking 時代錯誤. Let's look into the history of this one:

The first and second kanji (時代) form a very common compound that means "period," "epoch" or "era."

The third kanji (錯) means "confused" or "to be in disorder."

The fourth kanji (誤) means "mistake," or "to err," so it connects with 錯 to mean "fall into error." Usually, someone's old-fashioned way of thinking is what brands as a 時代錯誤, rather than their fashion.

このばあいは、時代錯誤とコスプレのちがいがわたしにはわからない。
In this case, it's hard to draw a line between anachronism and cosplay.

Fall Seven Times, Get Up Eight

七　転　八　起

しち　　てん　　はっ　　き

The red-hooded daruma doll is found in nearly every Japanese home. His round, heavy-centered body means he'll weeble and wobble, but he'll never fall down. This symbol of perseverance is the very embodiment of 七転八起.

The first kanji (七) is the number "seven."

The second kanji (転) means "to turn around" or "change."

The third kanji (八) is the number "eight."

The fourth kanj (起) means "to get up," which is literally what a daruma does in the face of defeat. In Japan, when you have a big task ahead of you (such as a school entrance exam), you paint in one of the daruma's eyes. Once you've persisted and reached your goal, you get to paint in the other eye.

ゆめをかなえたかったら、だるまのように七転八起しなきゃいけないね。

To make your dreams happen, you have to be like a daruma and get up after every fall.

Writhe In Agony

さ し す せ そ

七　転　八　倒

しち　てん　ばっ　とう

OUCH! He must've eaten one funky slice of sashimi. Whether it was just a bad piece of fish or something worse, this condition can only be described as 七転八倒. Forget the daruma on the previous page for a moment — sometimes, you fall down and stay down. Let's examine this kanji condition:
The first kanji (七) is the number "seven."
The second kanji (転) means to "turn around" or "change."
The third kanji (八) is the number "eight."
The fourth kanji (倒) means to "to collapse" or "break down," and though it's the only kanji that differs from 七転八起, it completely reverses the meaning: in this case, instead of getting back up, you collapse in a crumpled heap.

しょくちゅうどくで、おなかがいたくて七転八倒した。
He's was writhing in pain after getting food poisoning.

Sturdy And Simple

さしすせそ

質 実 剛 健

（しつ）（じつ）（ごう）（けん）

A true karate master is at peace with himself and the world around him.
He radiates strength, but without threat. Getting there requires determination,
but once he's made it, he can achieve the Zen-like state of 質実剛健.
The first kanji （質） means "quality."
The second kanji （実） means "truth," and with 質 indicates "simplicity."
The third kanji （剛） means "strength" or "sturdy."
The fourth kanji （健） means "health," and when combined with 剛 the two
become "vigor" and "virility," but 質実剛健 doesn't end at describing people.
Anything from a simple, sturdy piece of furniture to your unwavering desire to
study kanji can be described with this versatile phrase.

おしゃれではないけど質実剛健ないいおとこだ。
He may not be cool but he's a sturdy and simple man.

叱 咤 激 励

しっ　た　げき　れい

Sometimes the only thing you need to get out of a slump is a pep talk from your best friend. Of course, if he tells you everything you did wrong in a big, booming voice in front of the class, his words may have the opposite effect! This contradiction though, is where you'll find the true meaning of 叱咤激励:

The first and second kanji (叱咤) form a compound that means "scolding."
The third kanji (激) means "violent" or "to get excited."
The fourth kanji (励) means "to encourage," and together with 激 means "encouragement." As you can see this four-part 四字熟語 is another 対義語 (たいぎご) that combines the seemingly opposite words "reprimand" and "encouragement" to create a concept with a much broader meaning.

おおどりでせんぱいに叱咤激励されて、ちょっとはずかしかった。
It was a little embarrassing to get a pep talk from a senior right there on the street.

Surrounded By Enemies

し　めん　そ　か

Sometimes, it's not just paranoia – they really *are* out to get you! This situation can be called 四面楚歌, and the reason behind it is a true history lesson:

The first kanji (四) is the number "four"

The second kanji (面) means "face," and with 四 means "all sides."

The third kanji (楚) refers to the Chu Kingdom of ancient China. Enemies sang Chu folk songs to make the imperial army homesick during battle.

The fourth kanji (歌) means "song," and combined with 楚 becomes "chuge," or Chu folk songs. Even though this is one of the oldest 四字熟語 in the book, the phrase is used today in any situation where one is unanimously opposed or ignored – or outnumbered by invaders from a faraway land!

しあいであいてのおうえんせきにすわってしまい、四面楚歌のきぶんだった。
I felt surrounded by enemies when I mistakenly sat on the other team's side at the game.

Survival Of The Fittest

弱　肉　強　食

じゃく　　　にく　　　きょう　　　しょく

さしすせそ

That worm looks awfully happy when you consider that the chick next to it is probably about to eat it. While the chick is probably thrilled to have found dinner, it doesn't seem to realize it's about to become dinner, too. At least that sly cat is keeping a wary eye on the lion - he knows it's a jungle out there, where 弱肉強食 is the rule. Let's see if we can survive this one:

The first kanji (弱) means "weak."

The second kanji (肉) means "meat."

The third kanji (強) means "strong."

The third kanji (食) means "to eat." So, to put it bluntly, "the strong eat the meat of the weak."

どうぶつしゃかいだけでなく、にんげんしゃかいも弱肉強食である。

"Survival of the fittest" applies not only to the animal world, but the human one too.

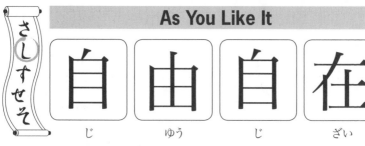

自 由 自 在
じ ゆう じ ざい

There's nothing like a little witchcraft when it comes to getting what you want — just about any goodie with the flick of the wand! Now that's what we call 自由自在. Let's summon the elements that make up this one:

The first and second kanji (自由) form a very common word that means "freedom" or "liberty."

The third kanji (自) is the same as the first, but alone it means "oneself."

The fourth kanji (在) is very rarely used alone, but is often used in conjunction with other kanji as it means "located in" or "exists," hence 自在 means "at will." This compound can also be used as an adjective, so if someone has full control over something, you might say their skills are 自由自在.

まほうがつかえたら、すきなものが自由自在にてにはいるのになぁ。
If I could use magic, I'd be able to get anything I want, whenever I want...

Different Strokes For Different Folks

十	人	十	色
じゅう	にん	と	いろ

You're studying a foreign language, so you know the world is filled with all kinds of different people. But when all is said and done, we're all just a bunch of cats. Wait, that's not right... Umm, anyway, as you can see from these feline friends, they're all quite different — and it seems to work just fine. That's 十人十色.

The first kanji (十) is the number "ten."
The second kanji (人) means "person."
The third kanji (十) is the same as the first, but this time is pronounced と.
The fourth kanji (色) means "color." The phrase 色々 (いろいろ) literally means "many colors," but when used in conversation it means "various." So we have ten colors – or ten variations – for ten people.

おなじようにそだてても十人十色、せいかくがまったくちがう。
Even though they were raised the same way, they've got totally different personalities.

酒池肉林

しゅ　ち　にく　りん

It's good to be the swami! This heavy-hitter is paying homage to the Di Xin, who ruled China under the Shang Dynasty from 1075-1046 BC and was the originator of the phrase 酒池肉林. Let's peek inside this party:

The first kanji（酒）means "alcohol."

The second kanji（池）means "lake."

The third kanji（肉）means "meat."

The fourth kanji（林）means "forest." If you can believe it, Di Xin was known for having parties where he'd fill a pool with liquor and then drape lots of meat on nearby trees, creating a literal 酒池肉林. Now that was a man who knew how to throw a bash!

このおうさまはまいよの酒池肉林のおかげで、メタボやばくない？

Check out the spare tire on that king — that's what he gets for living high on the hog.

Smooth Sailing

順風満帆

じゅん　　ぷう　　まん　　ぱん

Ahoy mateys! Ready for the voyage of... life? This versatile phrase has its roots in nautical communication, but has much broader usages today. This man's life for instance, would be described as 順風満帆 because it has proceeded in harmonious and trouble-free way.

The first kanji (順) means "order."
The second kanji (風) means "wind," and with 順 it means "favorable wind."
The third kanji (満) means "full" or "enough."
The fourth kanji (帆) means "the sail of a ship," so when combined with 満 it means "full sail." As you can see, this saying really does mean "smooth sailing," but you don't have to be a sailor to use it, as the picture shows.

おやはじぶんのこどもが順風満帆なせいかつをおくることをねがってる。
Parents just want to be able to give their children a smooth ride through life.

Gobbledygook

支離滅裂

し　り　めつ　れつ

Kaerblagh! Yigrblrgrg! Norborgorb! No matter how you pronounce it, it's about as much Japanese as it is English. Sometimes, being a native speaker just won't help. Either they can't understand you or you can't understand them, and you may as well be speaking different languages – even if you're not. The problem is, you're just speaking 支離滅裂!

The first kanji (支) means "support," or "sustain."

The second kanji (離) means "to detach," or "separate."

The third and fourth kanji (滅裂) mean "in chaos," which is what happens to your words when they turn into total gibberish! But don't worry, even world leaders have been known to devolve into 支離滅裂 every now and then.

かれはあまりのショックで、支離滅裂でなにをいっているのかわからない。
He's in such shock, I can't understand the gobbledegook he's blurting out.

Change Of Heart

心 機 一 転

しん　　き　　いっ　　てん

Check out our friend here. One moment, he was skulking through the day, the next he was a man of action. That can happen when you have a 心機一転. Let's look into this one – before we have our own change of heart:

The first kanji (心) means "heart" or "spirit."

The second kanji (機) means "machine" and combines with 心 to mean "the workings of one's heart," or more figuratively, "one's mental state or attitude."

The third kanji (一) is the number "one."

The fourth kanji (転) means "to turn around" or "change," and 一転 means "a complete change." Another meaning to 心機一転 is "to turn over a new leaf," so if you've gotten lazy in your kanji studies, now is a good time to start anew!

きょうからしごとがいそがしくなるぞ〜、心機一転がんばらなきゃ。
Work's gonna be busy from today on, I better have a change of heart and do my best.

Make A Mountain Out Of A Molehill

しん　　　しょう　　　ぼう　　　だい

This guy tells quite a story. Earlier, he came across a happy little puppy, but when he runs into his friend he just can't help but exaggerate that simple tale a bit. The amazing thing is how his friend actually believes him. They can't be close, otherwise he would know all about this guy's reputation for 針小棒大.

The first kanji (針) means "needle."

The second kanji (小) means "small" or "little."

The third kanji (棒) means "rod" or "pole."

The fourth kanji (大) means "big." This 四字熟語 is one of those cases where the construction closely resembles its English counterpart. While we make mountains out of molehills, the Japanese make poles out of needles.

かれがもりでオオカミにであったというはなしは、針小棒大じゃない？
Doesn't his story about meeting a wolf in the forest sound a little exaggerated?

Between A Rock And A Hard Place

絶 体 絶 命

ぜっ　たい　ぜつ　めい

It looks like Mustache Jiro's days are numbered, and in a few moments he'll have to choose between sleeping in a jail cell — or with the fishes out in Tokyo Bay! Either way, this bad guy is caught in a 絶体絶命.
The first kanji (絶) means "to discontinue" or "to sever."
The second kanji (体) means "body."
The third and fourth kanji (絶命) form a compound that means "the end of life," with 命 by itself meaning "fate" or "destiny." Make no mistake, you don't have to stare death in the face to experience this 四字熟語, though it literally means "the end of one's body and one's life." Getting caught reading comics in class is just as much of a 絶体絶命.

まて、くちひげじろう！ おまえはもう絶体絶命だ！
Wait, Mustache Jiro! You're really caught between a rock and a hard place now!

Derring-do

大　胆　不　敵
だい　たん　ふ　てき

Criminal mastermind Top-Hat Takahashi's unthinkable heists, daring escapes, and slick calling cards that feature photos of himself in the act put two-bit thieves like Mustache Jiro to shame! Top-Hat's secret is 大胆不敵 — a bold and fearless attitude. Let's approach this one carefully:

The first and second kanji (大胆) together mean "bold" or "audacious," with the second kanji 胆 meaning both "pluck" and "gall-bladder," so it's kind of like saying "guts" in English.

The third kanji (不) isn't a word by itself, but negates whatever comes after it.

The fourth kanji (敵) means "enemy," and the compound 不敵 means "fearless."

このけいびのなかから大胆不敵にダイヤをぬすむなんて、あいつしかいない！
Only he has the derring-do to steal a diamond from such a well guarded area!

A Great Selection

多 種 多 様

た　　しゅ　　た　　よう

There are two ways to buy shampoo. You can pick the least expensive — or cafefully select one from among the hundreds of varieties available. Choice isn't always a bad thing, and in many cases it can be fantastic to have a 多種多様. Let's see if we can clear it up with a little kanji lather:

The first kanji (多) means "many."

The second kanji (種) means "kind" or "variety."

The third kanji (多) is the same as the first.

The fourth kanji (様) means "manner" or "variety." In general you can add this compound to any noun to show that it is varied. 多種多様 is so versatile that you have at least as many ways to use it as there are shampoos on this shelf.

多種多様で、どれをえらんでいいかわからない！
There's such a great selection, I don't know which one to choose!

中途半端

ちゅう　と　はん　ぱ

This kid can't finish a bag of chips, let alone his homework! Every time he starts something, he stops in the middle to do something else. He better study these kanji or teachers will complain about how he leaves everything 中途半端:

The first kanji (中) means "middle."
The second kanji (途) means "route," or "way," so 中途 means "half-way."
The third kanji (半) means "half."
The fourth kanji (端) means "verge," and "end," so it combines with 半 to mean "fragment" or "incompleteness." This phrase is very common, and you can also use it to describe things you just didn't have time to finish, not just when you deliberately blow it off to play video games.

こら～！なんでも中途半端にしないの！
Hey! Stop leaving everything half-finished!

Rush Headlong

猪　突　猛　進

ちょ　とつ　もう　しん

たちってと

While a trained zoologist might use this expression to talk about the charge of a wild boar, the average Japanese speaker would probably say 猪突猛進 is what humans are like when they make hasty decisions, and don't stop until they've seen them through. Being pigheaded isn't all bad though; you can also rush headlong into a positive endeavor — like studying kanji!

The first kanji (猪) is indeed the kanji for "boar."

The second kanji (突) means "to thrust" or "to pierce," but when it follows 猪 they form a compound that means "recklessness."

The third kanji (猛) means "fierce" or "to become furious."

The fourth kanji (進) means "to proceed" or "to advance."

もくてきをはたすまでは、いのししのように猪突猛進でがんばるぞ〜
I'm gonna charge head-first like a boar until I achieve my goal!

Lightning Fast

電 光 石 火

でん　こう　せ　っか

It's good to get out of his way – if you even see him coming. No one even knows his name, because he never stops to talk. He's a perpetual motion machine, or maybe just 電光石火. Let's slow down long enough to figure it out:

The first kanji (電) means "electricity."

The second kanji (光) means "to shine," and in this case it forms a compound with 電 to mean "a flash of lightning or "an electric flash."

The third kanji (石) means "rock."

The fourth kanji (火) means "fire" and together with the third kanji means "sparks from hitting a flint." This 四字熟語 is useful for describing anything that's fast, from the shinkansen to the service at your favorite restaurant.

ちこくしそうなので、電光石火がっこうまではしる。
It looks like I'm gonna be late for school... I better run as fast as lighting.

Act Of God

天 変 地 異

てん　ぺん　ち　い

In Japan, nature has a tendency to show its rough side. The country is home to some of the world's most active volcanos, is prone to earthquakes, and gets hit regularly by typhoons — the worst of which are called 天変地異.

The first kanji (天) means "heaven."

The second kanji (変) means "strange" and can also be the verb "to change." The character forms a word with 天 that connotes heavy rain, snow, lightning and other acts of nature originating in the sky.

The third kanji (地) means "earth."

The fourth kanji (異) means "unusual," and forms a compound with 地 that covers all natural disasters on the ground — earthquakes, volcanoes, etc.

しまったー！おれのほけんは天変地異のばあいはむこうだ！！
Oh no! My insurance policy doesn't cover Acts of God!!

得　意　満　面

とく　い　まん　めん

You can tell this guy is as proud as a peacock. As if the trophy weren't enough, his smug expression just screams 得意満面. Let's grab the scent of this one:

The first and second kanji (得意) form a compound that means "triumph," "pride" and "strong point."

The third kanji (満) means "full" or "enough," and often precedes words to mean that something is "full" or "complete."

The fourth kanji (面) means "face," so when preceded by 満 it has the meaning "the whole face." His nose describes another expression, 天狗の鼻 (てんぐのはな), which means your pride is shown through your long nose, like that of the tengu (a Japanese goblin with a massive schnoz).

かれのかおは得意満面で、てんぐのはなになっている。
He's so proud of himself he's getting a nose like a tengu.

One Or The Other

二者択一

に　　しゃ　　たく　　いつ

なにぬねの

It may only be a friendly game of "Pick the Joker," but the tension can be high when the loser has to buy the ice cream! Well, at least it's only a 二者択一 situation, so the odds are even.

The first kanji (二) is the number "two."

The second kanji (者) means "someone," but when next to 二 it can mean either "two people" or "two things."

The third kanji (択) means "choose" or "select."

The fourth kanji (一) is the number "one." 二者択一 can also mean mean "the other of two choices," so even if that gal chooses the wrong card, she can use this alternate phrase to say that she meant to pick the other card!

この二者択一はわたしのじんせいをきめるわけではないけど・・・まけたくない！
It's not like this choice will decide my fate in life... I just don't wanna lose!

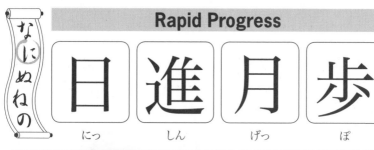

なにぬねの

日 進 月 歩

にっ　しん　げっ　ぽ

Hiroshi's hometown was just a farming village when he was growing up, but in a short time the rice paddies were transformed into skyscrapers — an example of the 日進月歩 of the modern age. Let's make some progress of our own:

The first kanji (日) means "sun" and "day," and it's also used to count days.
The second kanji (進) means "to proceed" or "to advance."
The third kanji (月) means "moon," but also "month."
The fourth kanji (歩) means "to walk," and is also a counter for steps. This is a kind of compound where its key words, 日月 (じつげつ; time) and 進歩 (しんぽ; progress) are written out of order.

つきりょこうは日進月歩でふかのうではないとおもう。
With enough rapid progress, I think one day we'll be able to travel to the moon.

Smile From Ear To Ear

破 顔 一 笑

は　　がん　　いっ　　しょう

Since most babies can't talk and certainly can't write kanji, they generally have no outlet to express themselves beyond cries, coos and facial expressions. But it's easy to tell how baby Amane is feeling with a 破顔一笑 like that. Like "side-splitting," this lighthearted phrase has an interesting kanji component you might not expect:

The first kanji (破) means "to tear" or "to destroy."

The second kanji (顔) means "face" or "expression," and it combines with 破 to mean "a broad smile."

The third and fourth kanji (一笑) link up to mean "a laugh." Let's hope little Amane learns to take care of the rest of life's travails with that great 破顔一笑.

あまねちゃんの破顔一笑は、みんなのくうきをあかるくする。
Just seeing Amane-chan smile from ear to ear makes everyone brighten up.

Everybody's Friend

八　方　美　人

はっ　　ぽう　　び　　じん

You can't please everyone — but he sure is trying, even if it means giving up his own integrity to do it. Sure he's has gone on 37 dates since last Tuesday, but it's not because he likes it, he just wants to be 八方美人. If he took a minute for himself to learn these kanji, he might think twice before date #38:

The first kanji (八) is the number "eight."

The second kanji (方) means "direction," and when preceded by 八 it has the meaning of "all directions."

The third and fourth kanji (美人) form a very common compound that means "a beautiful person," which is how this busy office boy wants to appear to others.

あのえいぎょうマンは八方美人すぎて、しんようできない。
That worker tries too hard to be everybody's friend — you can't trust him.

Always On Target

百　発　百　中

ひゃっ　　ぱつ　　ひゃく　　ちゅう

In Japan, darts isn't just a barroom pastime. In fact, you can play at any family amusement center. And from the looks of it, this kid is a regular – his darts are 百発百中. Let's take aim at this one:

The first kanji（百）is the number "100."

The second kanji（発）means "to discharge" or "depart," so after 百 it means "100 shots," referring to darts, bullets or any other projectile.

The third kanji（百）is the same is the same as the first, "100."

The fourth kanji（中）means "middle" or "center." This expression probably has its roots in traditional archery, but nowadays is used for any projectile, and can also refer to someone who is never wrong.

かれのうでまえは百発百中、こんどのしあいでもゆうしょうさ。
His skills are always on target, he'll win the next match for sure.

Live Long And Prosper

ふ　ろう　ちょう　じゅ

Chinese philosopher Lao Tsu's name means "old master," but you won't find him in any retirement home. It seems he's found the secret to 不老長寿, and maybe you can too once you learn the true nature of this expression:
The first kanji (不) is a particle that negates whatever comes after it.
The second kanji (老) means "to grow old," and when connected to 不 it means "eternal youth."
The third kanji (長) means "long."
The fourth kanji (寿) by itself means "one's natural life." If 寿 looks familiar to you, it may be because it is also the す in 寿司（すし）sushi, which is part of the healthy diet that is said to be one reason Japanese live so long.

いがくのはったつで不老長寿のくすりができるかもしれない。
With medical advances, we may someday see a drug that promises eternal life.

Master Of Disguise

変 幻 自 在

へん　げん　じ　ざい

はひふへほ

According to Japanese legend, tanuki (racoon dogs) and foxes have the power to change their appearance at will, and masquerade as anything from people to statues to pull pranks on each other. 変幻自在 isn't just for magical woodland animals, though:

The first kanji (変) means "unusual" and "to change"

The second kanji (幻) means "phantasm," "dream" or "illusion," and together with the first kanji forms a compound 変幻 meaning "transformation."

The third and fourth kanji (自在) together mean "at will." A slightly more realistic example of 変幻自在 would be a professional athlete who can play any position, or an actor who plays 10 characters in a one-man show.

かのじょのぶたいは、きつねとたぬきのように変幻自在にいしょうをかえる。
In their show, the actresses change their outfits like a tanuki or fox changes form.

Lose Yourself

無 我 夢 中

む が む ちゅう

J-Pop fans know that live shows beat mp3's anyday. Surrounded by hoards of fans, yet almost close enough to touch the dreamy musicians on stage, it's hard not to feel 無我夢中. These kanji lyrics can make anyone swoon:
The first kanji (無) is not a word but a particle, and it means "none."
The second kanji (我) means "I" or "oneself."
The third kanji (夢) is ゆめ by itself and it means dream.
The fourth kanji (中) means "middle" or "center," and so after 夢 it forms a compound that means "trance" or "engrossment." This phrase is mostly used when you are infatuated with someone or something, but for the narcissists out there, you can also say you are 無我夢中 about yourself!

コンサートでは、無我夢中でみんなのめがハートになった。
Everyone lost themselves at the concert and their eyes turned into hearts.

In Peak Physical Condition

無　病　息　災

む　びょう　そく　さい

まみむめも

Talk about being energetic! This kid is so healthy that germs, viruses and allergens bounce right off him. Let's hope he shares whatever vitamins he's taking, because they are keeping him 無病息災. Here's the prescription:

The first kanji (無) is not a word but a particle, and it means "none."

The second kanji (病) means "ill" or "sick," and forms a compound with 無 that means "in sound health."

The third and fourth kanji (息災) are a little tricky, because a modern reader might see 息 (いき; breath) with 災い (わざわい; cursed or disaster) and assume a negative meaning. However, the compound 息災 is actually a very old Buddhist term meaning to "be protected from disease."

じんじゃで、無病息災をねがってからけんこうになった。
Ever since praying at the shrine for protection, I've been in peak physical condition.

優　柔　不　断

ゆう　じゅう　ふ　だん

No, it's not that every item offered at Danny's fine Western dining is so delectable that it's impossible to make a choice – it's just that this girl is incredibly indecisive, or 優柔不断. Never mind that the ham dinner, ham special and ham surprise are all the same thing. Here's the menu for this one:

The first and second kanji (優柔) both have the meaning of "tenderness" and "gentleness" and form a compound meaning "half-hearted" or "indecisive."

The third kanji (不) is a particle that negates whatever comes after it.

The fourth kanji (断) means "judgement," which is exactly what this customer can't do. If this is how she handles dinner decisions, what do you think happens when she faces a real dilemma?

優柔不断なおきゃくさんにはこまるよね～。
Customers that can never decide are such a pain.

Making A List, Checking It Twice

用　意　周　到

よう　い　しゅう　とう

Taking a cue from santa, Hiro is checking his list not twice - but three or four times. You'd think he was heading off on a long expedition, and not a weekend camping trip. But Hiro can't help himself – he's got 用意周到 in his veins. Take a look at this one, and then come back and read it again:

The first kanji (用) means "use" or "to utilize."

The second kanji (意) means "thought" or "idea," and forms a very common compound 用意 meaning "preparation."

The third kanji (周) means "circumference" or "a lap."

The fourth kanji (到) means "arrival" or "reach," so it connects with 周 to mean "meticulous," "careful," or literally: "thorough going."

わたしはじしんにそなえ、いつでも用意周到である。
I am always very thoroughly prepared in the event of an earthquake.

Four-Character Compound

四字熟語

よ　じ　じゅく　ご

Both the topic and the title of this book, 四字熟語 isn't actually a 四字熟語 in every sense of the word because it's just a noun. But it is a four-character compound that's used throughout this book, so let's learn what it means:

The first kanji (四) is the number "four."

The second kanji (字) means "a character," "letter" or "word" and with 四 becomes an abbreviation of 四文字 (よんもじ) meaning "four characters."

The third kanji (熟) means "ripen" or "mature."

The fourth kanji (語) means "word" or "language," and combines with 熟 to mean both "conjunction" and "idiom." Many 四字熟語 originated from Chinese phrases called 成語 (cheng yu), most of which were four characters.

よっつのかんじでぶんしょうをあらわす四字熟語はすごいね。
It's amazing that you can express a whole sentence in just four kanji using yojijukugo.

Making A Name For Yourself

立　身　出　世

りっ　しん　しゅつ　せ

Move to Tokyo and can't get a job? Don't feel down, just take a picture of yourself suited up in front of Japan's Diet (parliament) building to send home to the folks! Your name will become synonymous with 立身出世. Here's why:

The first kanji (立) means "to stand up."

The second kanji (身) means "somebody" and "one's station in life," so it forms a compound with 立 that means "establishing oneself in life."

The third kanji (出) means "to leave" or "to exit."

The fourth kanji (世) means "the world" or "society," and so 出世 means "a promotion" or "a successful career." Starting to feel ambitious? Good, because Japanese speeches are filled with — you guessed it — 四字熟語!

かれはちいさいころからゆうしゅうだったから、立身出世はまちがいなし。
He's been tops since childhood, there's no doubt he'll be making a name for himself.

らりるれろ

老若男女

ろう　にゃく　なん　にょ

With something for everyone to do, see, and of course eat, local festivals are truly 老若男女 events. Let's see how these kanji bring the family together:
The first kanji (老) means "to grow old."
The second kanji (若) is read わかい by itself and it means "young."
The third kanji (男) is read おとこ by itself and means "male."
The fourth kanji (女) is read おんな by itself and means "female." If you know the kanji used in this 四字熟語 already, you might know that the standard *on* reading would be ろうじゃくだんじょ. However, this particular 四字熟語 is a holdover from the Wu Dynasty, which used a different pronunciation. Today you can use either pronunciation, old or new, a testament to the idiom's meaning.

このえいがは老若男女だれにでもたのしめるね。
This movie has something for everyone; it's fun for the whole family.

和 洋 折 衷

わ よう せつ ちゅう

Check out this crazy cultural mix. Her outfit is part Wild West, part 和風 (わふう; Japanese-style). That teriyaki burger alone can be called 和洋折衷. It might be Japanese, but these kanji definitely cross some cultural borders:

The first kanji (和) usually means "harmony" and "peace," but in this case it means "Japanese style."

The second kanji (洋) is used to mean "western-style."

The third kanji (折) means "to fold" or "fracture."

The fourth kanji (衷) means "heart" or "mind," and so it creates a compound with 折 that means "a compromise" or "blending." It may be an ancient term, but today 和洋折衷 is everywhere. You reading this book is a good example!

かのじょのかっこうだけではなく、このてりやきバーガーまで和洋折衷だ。
It isn't just her outfit, she's east-meets-west right up to the teriyaki burger in her hand.

kanji de Manga

**HIRAGANA
AND KATAKANA
CHARTS**

The 46 Basic
HIRAGANA
Each character represents one syllable

あ a	い i	う u	え e	お o
か ka	き ki	く ku	け ke	こ ko
さ sa	し shi	す su	せ se	そ so
た ta	ち chi	つ tsu	て te	と to
な na	に ni	ぬ nu	ね ne	の no
は ha	ひ hi	ふ fu	へ he	ほ ho
ま ma	み mi	む mu	め me	も mo
や ya		ゆ yu		よ yo
ら ra	り ri	る ru	れ re	ろ ro
わ wa				を o
				ん n

The 46 Basic
KATAKANA

Each character represents one syllable

ア a	イ i	ウ u	エ e	オ o
カ ka	キ ki	ク ku	ケ ke	コ ko
サ sa	シ shi	ス su	セ se	ソ so
タ ta	チ chi	ツ tsu	テ te	ト to
ナ na	ニ ni	ヌ nu	ネ ne	ノ no
ハ ha	ヒ hi	フ fu	ヘ he	ホ ho
マ ma	ミ mi	ム mu	メ me	モ mo
ヤ ya		ユ yu		ヨ yo
ラ ra	リ ri	ル ru	レ re	ロ ro
ワ wa				ヲ o
				ン n

Contracted
HIRAGANA

A small や, ゆ or よ can be added to any character that ends in an "i" vowel (except for the character い itself) to form a contracted sound, as shown here.

きゃ kya	きゅ kyu	きょ kyo
しゃ sha	しゅ shu	しょ sho
ちゃ cha	ちゅ chu	ちょ cho
にゃ nya	にゅ nyu	によ nyo
ひゃ hya	ひゅ hyu	ひょ hyo
みゃ mya	みゅ myu	みょ myo
りゃ rya	りゅ ryu	りょ ryo
ぎゃ gya	ぎゅ gyu	ぎょ gyo
じゃ ja	じゅ ju	じょ jo
びゃ bya	びゅ byu	びょ byo
ぴゃ pya	ぴゅ pyu	ぴょ pyo

Contracted
KATAKANA

A small ヤ, ユ or ヨ can be added to any character that
ends in an "i" vowel (except for the character イ itself)
to form a contracted sound, as shown here.

キャ kya	キュ kyu	キョ kyo
シャ sha	シュ shu	ショ sho
チャ cha	チュ chu	チョ cho
ニャ nya	ニュ nyu	ニョ nyo
ヒャ hya	ヒュ hyu	ヒョ hyo
ミャ mya	ミュ myu	ミョ myo
リャ rya	リュ ryu	リョ ryo
ギャ gya	ギュ gyu	ギョ gyo
ジャ ja	ジュ ju	ジョ jo
ビャ bya	ビュ byu	ビョ byo
ピャ pya	ピュ pyu	ピョ pyo

Two-Dash and One-Circle
HIRAGANA AND KATAKANA

To modify the sounds of certain kana,
add two small dashes (called dokuten)
or a tiny circle (called a handakuten)

が ga	ぎ gi	ぐ gu	げ ge	ご go
ざ za	じ ji	ず zu	ぜ ze	ぞ zo
だ da	ぢ ji	づ zu	で de	ど do
ば ba	び bi	ぶ bu	べ be	ぼ bo
ぱ pa	ぴ pi	ぷ pu	ぺ pe	ぽ po

ガ ga	ギ gi	グ gu	ゲ ge	ゴ go
ザ za	ジ ji	ズ zu	ゼ ze	ゾ zo
ダ da	ヂ ji	ヅ zu	デ de	ド do
バ ba	ビ bi	ブ bu	ベ be	ボ bo
パ pa	ピ pi	プ pu	ペ pe	ポ po

INDEX

INDEX OF YOJIJUKUGO

The 80 yojijukugo featured in this special edition of *Kanji de Manga* are in Japanese syllabary order. They are indexed here based on their English definitions.

MOE USA
Volume 2: Costume Crisis
By Atsuhisa Okura
ISBN-10: 4-921205-19-1 ISBN-13: 978-4-921205-19-5
Paperback. English. 160 b/w pages. 5 inches x 7 inches.
US $9.99, CAN $11.99, UK £6.50

Patty-chan and Ruby-chan are back in action in the second installment!
This time, the girls are in a topsy-turvy search for the magical maid
costumes that were stolen from them just before their big concert at
Tokyo's Budokan. They've enlisted the services of a super-secret
organization — the Akihabara Otaku Network — to help them track down
the theif and rescue their careers. But have they met their match?

MANGA SISTERS
By Saori Takarai & Misato Takarai
ISBN-10: 4-921205-18-3 ISBN-13: 978-4-921205-18-8
Hardcover. English & Japanese 96 color pages. 5 inches x 5 inches.
US $9.99, CAN $11.99, UK £6.50

Saori and Misato Takarai know exactly what it means to be "Manga
Sisters." The two artists grew up in Tokyo and, like most siblings, learned
how to be both competitive and compassionate as they dealt with
parents, teachers, boyfriends and — perhaps most difficult of all — each
other. Now they share their secrets of manga sisterhood in this delightful
new illustrated book from Manga University.

THE MANGA COOKBOOK
By The Manga University Culinary Institute & Chihiro Hattori
ISBN-10: 4-921205-07-08 ISBN-13: 978-4-921205-07-2
Paperback. English. 160 pages (16 in color). 5.75 inches x 8 inches.
US $14.95, CAN $16.95, UK £9.99

Reading manga sure can make a person hungry! Food appears frequently
in Japanese comics, but what exactly is it that the characters are eating?
Introducing "The Manga Cookbook", an illustrated step-by-step guide to
preparing simple Japanese dishes using ingredients found in every
Western kitchen. Features 27 recipes and cultural notes.

SAMURAI CONFIDENTIAL
By Ryuto Kanzaki
ISBN-10: 4-921205-21-3 ISBN-13: 978-4-921205-21-8
Hardcover. English. 64 pages (10 in color). 7.5 inches x 10.25 inches.
US $19.95, CAN $21.95

Acclaimed Japanese storyteller and manga artist Ryuto Kanzaki makes
her English-language debut with *Samurai Confidential,* a sweeping
pictorial that showcases the private, often complex lives of Japan's most
famous samurai warriors. More than just a lavish picture book, though,
Samurai Confidential is rich with nuggest of information not normally
found in mainstream history books. From the Tokugawa Shogunate to the
final days of Edo, from Kenshin to Ieyasu to Musashi, *Samurai Confidential*
has all the bushi bases covered.

Purchase all these and much more from our online store
www.mangauniversity.com

GLENN KARDY is director of Japanime, an award-winning creative agency and publisher of Manga University's acclaimed lineup of educational materials. He lives in the Tokyo suburb of Kawaguchi City with his wife, their daughter and a collection of Oakland A's bobblehead dolls.

CHIHIRO HATTORI has been the featured artist in all eight volumes of the *Kana de Manga/Kanji de Manga* series, and she also illustrated Manga University's *Manga Cookbook*. Chihiro, her husband and their son live in Yokohama, where they enjoy fine food, fast cars, and high fashion.

Art coordinator: Mari Oyama
Translation and design: Naomi Rubin
Sales director: Chris Kardy
Editorial assistant: Eric Fischbach

Back cover illustration by MImei Sakamoto

Special thanks to Edward Mazza